Productivity

Productivity

Get motivated, get organized, and get things done

Gill Hasson

CAPSTONE
A Wiley Brand

This edition first published 2019.

© 2019 Gill Hasson

Registered office
John Wiley & Sons Ltd, The Atrium, Southern Gate, Chichester, West Sussex, PO19 8SQ, United Kingdom

For details of our global editorial offices, for customer services and for information about how to apply for permission to reuse the copyright material in this book please see our website at www.wiley.com.

Library of Congress Cataloging-in-Publication Data

Names: Hasson, Gill, author.
Title: Productivity : get motivated, get organised, and get things done / Gill Hasson.
Description: Chichester, West Sussex, United Kingdom : John Wiley & Sons, 2019. | Includes index. |
Identifiers: LCCN 2019007046 (print) | LCCN 2019007968 (ebook) | ISBN 9780857088017 (Adobe PDF) | ISBN 9780857088055 (ePub) | ISBN 9780857087843 (pbk.)
Subjects: LCSH: Time management. | Motivation (Psychology)
Classification: LCC BF637.T5 (ebook) | LCC BF637.T5 H37 2019 (print) | DDC 650.1—dc23
LC record available at https://lccn.loc.gov/2019007046

Cover Design: Wiley
Cover Image: © Ani_Ka/Getty Images

Set in 12/15pt SabonLTStd by SPiGobal, Chennai, India

Printed in Great Britain by TJ International Ltd, Padstow, Cornwall, UK

10 9 8 7 6 5 4 3 2 1

Harry, My clever boy.

Contents

Introduction

Being productive means making things happen and getting things done.

What being productive *doesn't* mean, though, is squeezing every minute out of every hour of every day to become some sort of productivity machine. Being productive doesn't mean working harder – it means working smarter; getting things done effectively and efficiently.

Do you want to get more done? Do you want to be able to fit more in? Or would you like to achieve more by doing less? Either way, what's stopping you? What's stopping you getting things done efficiently and effectively?

Perhaps you're doing too much. Perhaps you rush round in a state of panic; you've got too much to do and too much to think about. You can't think clearly; your head is full of what you're doing, what you haven't done, and what you've yet to do. You're certainly doing a lot, but you're not doing it efficiently.

On the other hand, it could be that you're not doing enough. You have things you want to get done but you get stuck; you find it difficult to get started, to keep going and get things finished. You don't feel like you ever get much done.

It doesn't have to be like this!

Chapter 1 starts by encouraging you to think about what your reasons might be; why you might be finding it difficult to be productive and get things done. Whatever it is that's getting in the way of you being more productive, it can be overcome. Chapter 1 explains how the way you think – your attitude and approach – makes all the difference. You need a productivity mindset: persistence, determination, and a positive, open mind; a willingness to be adaptable and flexible.

But as well as a productive mindset, it's important to recognize that what you *don't* do helps determine what you *can* do. Chapter 1 also encourages you to identify commitments and chores that may be cluttering up your time and preventing you from getting on with the things you really want to do.

You might, though, feel that you *should* be able to fit it all in – other people seem to manage, don't they? Well of course, there's always someone else you know or hear about who seems to be getting so much done – who's able to fit more into their days than you ever thought possible.

But that's their life, not yours.

If you look more closely, you'll find that productive people have set things up to succeed according to *their* skills, strengths, and abilities; *their* resources, interests, commitments, and obligations. And rather than working harder, they're working smarter.

You can do the same.

Chapter 2 explains the importance of identifying and drawing on your own skills, strengths, and abilities to help you to be productive; to get things done effectively and efficiently. Then, once you've looked at what's getting in the way and identified the attributes you already have that can help you be more productive, you can start getting yourself more organized. Chapter 3 tells you how.

You'll need to be clear about what it is that you want to get done – what areas and aspects of your life you want to be more productive in. Then, once you have a realistic idea about what, how much, and by when you want to get things done, the next thing to do is to plan how and when you'll do it.

Of course, when it comes to productivity and time management, there's nothing new about setting goals, planning, prioritizing, scheduling tasks, and having routines. But what *is* new is the approach described in this book to doing these things; to planning, prioritizing, etc.

Throughout this book, the emphasis is on the fact that productivity is personal: it involves finding your own rhythm and getting things done in a way that works best for *you;* according to *your* circumstances, *your* skills and abilities, and the time, energy and resources *you* have.

You might, for example, be someone who needs to tackle difficult tasks and irritating chores head on. On the other hand, you might prefer to ease into your day. Chapter 3 encourages you to be aware of when might be the optimum time of day for you to be productive.

You'll need to remain flexible and open to changing how you do things, because no matter how organized you are – how well you plan your time and your tasks – and how efficiently and effectively you do them, challenges and setbacks happen. You then have to let go of your plans. And plan again.

Having begun to look at why you might be struggling to be more productive in Chapter 1, Chapter 4 looks at what to do about those difficulties. One of the most common challenges is just getting started on things. For many of us, it's easy to keep putting things off. But the guilt and anxiety that you feel while procrastinating are often worse than the effort and energy you have to put into whatever it is that you're putting off doing!

The thing is, waiting until you *really* feel like doing something is a sure-fire way for things *not* to get done. In fact, it's normal *not* to feel like doing something in the beginning. So, what to do? Chapter 4 has a number of methods – ideas and suggestions – to help you overcome procrastination. It also has some suggestions to help make it easier to keep going; to persist when you come up against difficulties and challenges with whatever it is you're trying to get done.

There will always be setbacks, delays, and hold ups. When there are setbacks and difficulties, you need to refocus your attention on what you can do that could move things forward for you. If you really want to achieve something, there's usually a way. And most likely, there's more than one way.

Whether it's a major delay or a minor hold up, you'll need to know when to let go of what you can't control and look at what you *can* control. When you do that, you take a step towards getting back on track.

When things aren't going as well as you'd planned, one thing that can make a positive difference is to get help from others. In fact, trying to do everything yourself is not the best use of your time, skills, or energy; struggling for hours or days before finally getting help can leave you feeling overwhelmed and stressed. And then you can't do anything properly. Other people are often more willing to help than you might think. But if you don't ask, the answer is already no!

And yet, although other people can be of help, when it comes to being productive they can also be a hindrance. Chapter 5 explains how you can manage other people's interruptions; their demands and requests. In fact, learning to be more assertive – saying 'no' to other people's requests or tasks if you're too busy, if it is not that important, if someone else can handle it, or if it can be done later – is a key skill if you want to be more productive.

So is a balanced lifestyle. If you're going to give your best to being productive and getting things done, you need to aim for a balanced amount of work and rest in your life. Chapter 6 has some suggestions for how you can do this.

And finally, what, you might ask, qualifies me to write a book about being productive?

I don't make lists or have daily plans. I'm a morning person, I can't think straight after 6 p.m. I can't work in the evenings; I finish working by 6.30 p.m., cook dinner and watch TV most evenings. I don't have one place of work; sometimes I work from the kitchen table, other times I work sitting on the bed or on the sofa. And in the summer, when it's sunny, I'm squinting at my laptop screen in the garden.

I can't concentrate for more than an hour at a time. I'm easily distracted. (It's always been so. When I was nine years old, my teacher Miss Tibbles wrote in my school report that I was *'easily distracted by fun loving evils from across the room.'*)

My only routine is to write every day. It doesn't matter if it's only half an hour a day or six hours a day: unless I'm on holiday, I write every day.

I fit my work around my social life; meeting friends for lunch, days out, trail walking with my friend Gilly, holidays and weekends away with friends and family. I have yet to cancel a social engagement because I'm too busy. But by any measure, that hasn't stopped me from being productive, happy, and successful. As well as my social life, the voluntary work that I do and teaching a couple of times a week, I write an average of three books a year.

How come? I've worked out what works for me. If you want to be more productive, you need to do just that. This book will help!

1
What's Stopping You?

No doubt you're aware that by being more productive you'll improve yourself or your situation in some way; you'll be wealthier or wiser, happier, healthier, or less stressed. But whatever aspect of your life you're hoping to improve, one thing that's for sure is that being more productive means you'll be doing things effectively and efficiently; you won't be wasting time, effort, resources, or money. You'll feel more on top of things and more in control of your life.

But if you already know that being productive will improve your situation, what's stopping you? What's stopping you getting things done efficiently and effectively? There are a number of reasons why you might be struggling.

Which of these situations is familiar to you?

- I'm not always clear about what, exactly, I want to achieve.

- I'm not always clear about what does and doesn't need doing.
- I often have too much to do and don't know where to start or what to do next.
- For any one task or number of tasks, I don't plan out what I'm going to do. I just jump in.
- I have little in the way of structure and routine in my day.
- My time often gets cluttered with unimportant things.
- I spend too much time dealing with interruptions and distractions.
- I'm prone to procrastination; I keep putting off getting started.
- I'm indecisive.
- I tend to overthink what's to be done and I make things complicated.
- I have low expectations; I don't have much confidence in my abilities. I simply don't think I'm capable of achieving much in the way of being productive.
- I don't recognize and make use of my strengths.
- I tend to try and do things when I'm not at my best; when I'm tired or stressed.
- I have clear methods and routines that I stick to. I don't like to change or adapt them.
- I'm a perfectionist; I get hung up on details and I won't make compromises.
- I often underestimate the time, energy, and resources I need in order to get things done.

- I don't persist. When I come across problems and difficulties with what I'm trying to achieve, I give up too easily.
- I don't get help and support from other people.
- I'm stubborn! When I come across difficulties and challenges I carry on doing something despite the evidence that things aren't working out. I don't try and find a different way to get things done.

Whatever it is that's thwarting your attempts to be more productive – to get things done efficiently and effectively – the good news is that it *can* be overcome.

A Productive Mindset

When it comes to being productive, the way you think – your attitude and approach – makes all the difference. You need a productivity mindset.

The key characteristics of a productivity mindset are on the one hand, persistence and determination and on the other hand, a positive, open mind; a willingness to be adaptable and flexible.

Without persistence, not only do you achieve less than you're capable of, you don't get to discover what you *are* capable of achieving. And you don't get the confidence that comes from pushing through and eventually succeeding. Persistence provides its own momentum.

If you can just keep going, you'll eventually get results. And results motivate you to continue.

There's a difference, though, between being persistent and being stubborn. Being stubborn is being determined *not* to change your attitude or approach to doing something despite the evidence that things aren't working out.

But as Albert Einstein once said: 'Insanity is doing the same thing over and over again and expecting different results.' Being stubborn means it's less likely that you'll step back to get a broader perspective on what is and isn't happening and become more strategic. In contrast, when you're persistent, although you're determined to succeed, you can see when something is not working. You're flexible; you're able to adjust your plans and actions and are prepared to listen to suggestions, ideas, and advice. You're open to new ways of doing things so that you can keep moving forward, making things happen, and getting things done.

Admittedly, the line between stubbornness and persistence is thin and can be difficult to distinguish. But stubbornness leads to stagnation; it struggles on and it doesn't accept other possibilities, other ways of doing something. Persistence is a more uplifting experience; periods of difficulty are interspersed with small gains and measures of progress. These small gains inspire you and give you hope; you recognize and build on them.

It's likely that you've been both persistent and stubborn at some point in the past.

Think of a time when you've achieved something through persistence – passed your driving test, learnt to speak a language, play a musical instrument, or some other activity. No doubt it wasn't easy, but you achieved it because you were persistent; when things became difficult, you found a way to overcome the challenges and you moved forward.

Now think of a time when you clung onto something – a job or relationship. Rather than recognize it wasn't working out and that nothing was changing, you hung on in there. Or remember a time when you got lost walking or driving somewhere. Rather than ask someone for directions, you kept going but ended up even more lost. That was you being stubborn.

Stubbornness is delusional thinking. Persistence is positive thinking.

Having a positive outlook doesn't mean denying the challenges and difficulties of a situation. Rather, you acknowledge the difficulties and challenges and then, instead of letting them drag you down into a spiral of negative thinking, you move on to work out how you can now respond in positive, constructive ways. And you use the difficulties as learning experiences for the future.

Letting Go Of What's Not Important

So, to be more productive requires a productive mindset: persistence and determination and a positive, open mind;

a willingness to be adaptable and flexible. But before you can start doing anything, let's look at what you could stop doing.

Steve Jobs – the cofounder of Apple – once said that what made Apple Apple was not so much what they chose to build but all the projects they chose to ignore. It's true, what you *don't* do helps determine what you *can* do. For many of us, it's not that there's not enough time in the day; it's that we've got too many commitments getting in the way of doing the things we most want to do and really need to get done.

Maybe you're the sort of person who overcommits when you're feeling particularly enthusiastic and optimistic about what you're able to do. Or you just want to help someone out. At the time, when you decide to take it on, you think you'll be able to manage. You agree to more chores and tasks, errands, assignments, and projects. You take on more duties, responsibilities, and obligations.

Which of your commitments have become a burden? Whether it's a local cause or you've simply agreed to walk your neighbour's dog or look after their cat, you've taken on a new project or some extra work, or it's always you that does the coffee run, are there things you can drop so that you have more time for the important things? The things you really want to get done?

Of course, taking a step back and disengaging from some of your commitments isn't always easy. It may be that you're thinking about sunk costs; the time, effort, love, or money you've already put into something. Even though you now regret having got involved, instead of letting go, you struggle on.

Perhaps you tell yourself you just can't; you'll let people down if you drop out. You said you'd do something, so you feel obliged – you feel it's your duty – you should keep your word, stick with it, and put up with the difficulties. Or maybe you're worried about the response you'll get if you pull out; the other person will be upset or angry. You feel trapped, but you don't want to let people down and you can't face handling their reaction if you back out. And maybe you don't want to call it a day because you don't want to admit that you were wrong to have committed to it in the first place.

It doesn't have to be like this!

At the time you decided to get involved or to do something, you made the right choice. Now, however, you realize it's not what you want to do; you've had a change of heart; your feelings have changed and you realize it's getting in the way of what you'd rather be doing.

For each commitment, ask yourself: 'Is it that important to me; in line with what I really want to get done?'

Have courage! You may well feel concerned – worried and anxious – about telling someone else that you're going to stop doing whatever it is you said you'd do. That's ok – it's okay to feel some trepidation – but rather than focusing on how anxious you feel, think of how much better you'll feel for having taken action. Unless you signed a contract, there's nothing to stop you from walking away. You may feel uncomfortable – you've got to explain your change of mind to friends, family, or colleagues – but having a few uncomfortable conversations is a small price to pay for freeing yourself from commitments that are no longer of interest or that you don't have time for. Other people might need someone to fill your role but it doesn't have to be you. If you left the situation tomorrow – left the committee for example – in three months' time, what do you think would happen to those people who 'need' you? They'll adjust, and quite quickly they will be fine. People can and will sort it out. But if you stay in that situation because you think that you 'should' or you 'have to', in three months' time, will you be fine?

How to tell them? Just be honest, clear, and succinct. Avoid waffling, rambling, or giving excuses. Don't blame someone or something else, just be honest. You only need one genuine reason for saying no. Just say what you need to say. Say, for example, 'I'm sorry, I'm not going to be able to continue ...'. Or 'Next month I'm going to stop ...'. Once you've said what you've got to say, say no more. Just listen to the other person's response. Then acknowledge their response but stand your ground.

And the time, energy, or money you've already invested? That's all now in the past. Don't let the past dictate the present. Think about what you have to gain rather than what you have to lose by pulling out. If you can let go of some of the things you do, you'll feel less stressed and you'll have more time and energy for the things you really want to do.

Think like Beyonce. As she once said: 'Thank God I found the good in goodbye.'

Is there something or some things that you can let go of; not do, or not go to, or get someone else to do? (More about getting help from other people in Chapter 5.) Whatever it is, let it go knowing that what's left is more in line with what you need and want to do with your time.

In a nutshell

- Whatever it is that's thwarting your attempts to be more productive – to get things done efficiently and effectively – the good news is that it *can* be overcome.
- The way you think – your attitude and approach – makes all the difference. You need a productivity mindset: persistence and determination and a positive, open mind; a willingness to be adaptable and flexible.
- There's a difference between being persistent and being stubborn. Being stubborn is being determined *not* to change your attitude or approach to doing something despite the evidence that things aren't working out.

- But with persistence, although you're determined to succeed, you can see when something is not working. You're able to adjust your plans, are prepared to listen to ideas and advice, and are open to new ways of doing things so that you can keep moving forward to get things done.
- Stubbornness is delusional thinking. Persistence is positive thinking.
- What you *don't* do helps determine what you *can* do. Is there something or some things that can you let go not do, or not go to, or get someone else to do?
- Think about what you have to gain rather than what you have to lose by pulling out. If you can let go of some of the things you do, you'll feel less stressed and you'll have more time and energy for the things you really want to do.

2
Know Yourself

People who are productive – those who get things done – manage to do so not just because they have a productive mindset or because they've prioritized their commitments. They're effective and efficient because they draw on their skills, strengths, and qualities.

What skills do you have?

Maybe you have good written and verbal communication skills; you can clearly explain and understand ideas, opinions, thoughts, and feelings. You can clearly and succinctly tell others what does and doesn't need doing.

Perhaps you have good social and interpersonal skills; you can work cooperatively – listen to others, share ideas. You can be tactful and persuasive; you're skilled at negotiating, motivating, and encouraging others. Are you good at networking? If you do have good communication, social, and interpersonal skills, you can draw on those skills to work with others to be more productive – to be more efficient and effective in getting things done. (There's more about this in Chapter 5.)

Perhaps you have good research skills; you're good at finding relevant facts and information. Maybe you have good IT skills? Do you have any specific practical abilities? Perhaps you're skilled at using equipment and tools?

Any of these skills and abilities can support you in being productive; in getting things done more effectively and efficiently. Identify what they are so that you can exploit them to help you get things done.

Identify Your Qualities And Strengths

Read through this list and, as you do, tick *each and every* quality that applies to you.

- ☐ **Adaptable and flexible:** I'm able to change my approach and adjust to different conditions and circumstances.
- ☐ **Calm:** I can deal with problems as they happen; I don't get overexcited or too anxious, angry, or upset when things go wrong.
- ☐ **Conscientious:** I'm guided by a sense of what's right; I like to work carefully and do things thoroughly.
- ☐ **Cooperative:** I work well with other people; I'm willing to be of assistance in working towards a common goal.

□ **Decisive:** I make decisions easily, with little hesitation.

□ **Determined:** I resolve to stick to a decision and/or keep going.

□ **Enthusiastic:** I have a lively interest in ideas, activities, tasks, etc. I'm often eager to get on with things.

□ **Imaginative, creative, and innovative:** I can come up with new ways and ideas to make things happen and get things done and to solve problems and overcome difficulties.

□ **Intuitive and perceptive:** I'm insightful; I know when something does or doesn't feel right. I can read between the lines, pick up on what others are feeling, what their needs, likes, and dislikes are.

□ **Logical:** I'm capable of reasoning in a clear and consistent manner: I can easily work out what the next steps are.

□ **Methodical and organized:** I have clear methods and systems for doing things in an orderly way. I plan things efficiently.

□ **Observant:** I'm quick to notice things. I notice details and I'm perceptive.

□ **Open minded:** I'm willing to consider new ideas and different ways of doing things.

□ **Optimistic:** I am usually hopeful and confident that things will turn out well.

□ **Patient:** I can wait for things to happen in their own time. I can accept delays and difficulties without becoming annoyed or anxious.

□ **Persistent:** I can continue a course of action despite difficulty or opposition.

☐ **Practical and realistic:** I like to do whatever works; whatever is effective and brings results. I'm more concerned with the actual doing or use of something than with theory and ideas. I'm sensible and realistic in my approach to a situation or problem.

☐ **Reliable:** I can be trusted and depended on to keep my word, to do what I say I will, and to do something well.

☐ **Resilient:** I can recover quickly from adversity; from difficulties and setbacks.

☐ **Resourceful:** I'm able to find quick and clever ways to deal with new situations and overcome difficulties.

☐ **Responsible and accountable:** I can be trusted to do what I've said I'll do. Not only willing to ensure the job is done, but also accepting responsibility for the results – good or bad. I don't make excuses or lay blame if something doesn't work out. I can explain, justify, and take responsibility.

☐ **Thorough:** I take pains to do something carefully and completely.

Choose five of the qualities you've ticked. For each of those five qualities, think some more about how each quality has helped you in the past and can continue to help you be productive; to get things done effectively and efficiently.

For example, if you felt that patience was one of your qualities, you might recognize that at work you don't rush things or overlook details; you take time to do things properly so that you don't make mistakes and so you don't waste time having to go back over things.

If being imaginative and innovative are two of your strengths, you'll know that you can come up with new ways and ideas to make things happen and get things done. Can you think of times in the past when you've done that?

And if you're cooperative, you work well with other people. How do you think that's helped you be more productive – to be more effective and efficient at getting things done?

Know Your Learning Style

Being aware of your skills and strengths can help you feel more confident that you do have what it takes to be more productive. But did you know that as well as having specific skills, strengths, and qualities, you have your own individual way of learning? Imagine, for example, that you had to learn how to make, install, or mend something. Would you want to read the instructions first, think through each step, and then do it? Or would you just want to get stuck in and try different ways of doing something until you find the most successful?

The way the one person learns – takes in new ideas and information and acquires new knowledge and skills – may be different from the way you learn. Quite simply, some of us learn best by doing things first and then thinking about what we've learnt. Others learn best by thinking things through first and then getting on with the doing. When you're aware of how you learn best, you can use it to your advantage and apply your preferred approach to learning to help you be productive; to get things done more easily and efficiently.

In 1986, occupational psychologist Peter Honey and his colleague Alan Mumford, a management development advisor, identified four different learning styles: Activist, Pragmatist, Reflector, and Theorist. Not only can each of these learning styles be seen to apply to how a person learns, they also apply to how they approach tasks and activities and get things done. There are strengths and weaknesses to each style. The trick is to identify and make use of your strengths and to be aware of and work round your weaknesses.

If you're an Activist, you're someone who likes to get started on things straightaway. You're happy to hit the ground running. You love the challenge of new experiences and you'll try anything once. You're open-minded and enthusiastic about learning and doing new things. You learn best – and are therefore more productive – when you can just get on with it, without any constraints. However, you have a tendency to do too much yourself. You take unnecessary risks and rush into action without sufficient preparation. If things don't work out, instead of stopping to consider why, you often just move on to the next thing. You're impatient; you often don't consolidate – pull everything together at the end – and you leave things unfinished.

If your style of learning is that of a Pragmatist, once you've understood an idea or theory, you're keen to try it out and put it into practice. You learn best and are therefore more productive when you can solve problems, make practical decisions, and, like activists, get going on things. However, you may tend to seize on the first convenient solution to a problem and, although it might be practical, it may not always be the best, most suitable, or most appropriate way to get things done.

To be more productive – to be more efficient and effective at getting things done – Activists and Pragmatists need to work on:

- Planning and prioritizing.
- Listening to other's ideas and opinions and considering alternative ways forward.
- Reflecting on and learning from what worked and didn't work with any one task or project.
- Finding ways to stay engaged and persisting for longer periods.

If your preferred way of learning is that of a Theorist, you take a logical, structured approach to everything you learn and do. You like to analyse and understand the theory behind ideas, concepts, and systems. You're organized and disciplined and likely to be a perfectionist. However, you don't like uncertainty, disorder, and ambiguity. You're not happy until things fit into a rational scheme: a systematic and logical theory. Your perfectionism can result in procrastination; you hold back from doing something for fear of not being able to do it perfectly.

If your style of learning is that of a Reflector, you like to stand back, see things from different perspectives before doing anything. You're happy to observe and listen to others. You like harmony. You're ordered, careful, cautious, calm, methodical, and thorough. You learn best, and so therefore are more productive, if you can think first: do some research, gather views, opinions, ideas, and information. You like to do things in your own time without pressure and deadlines. You learn least, and so are least productive, when there's no time for planning and you don't have enough information to make a decision. You may have a tendency to procrastinate and you find it difficult to make short cuts.

When it comes to being more productive, Reflectors and Theorists may need to work on:

- Being more flexible.
- Being less of a perfectionist.
- Setting priorities and making decisions.
- Getting started on things.

You can find out for yourself what your preferred learning style is by Googling 'Honey and Mumford Learning Style Questionnaire'. You will probably find that you're not 100% any one particular learning style; that you prefer different methods of learning and doing things depending upon the situation.

It isn't that each of us can only learn or approach tasks and activities in one way, it's just that we might find one way easier and more effective than others. Honey and Mumford recommend that to maximize learning, we each need to understand our own learning style and seek out opportunities to learn and do things in the way that suits us best. But, just as importantly, we also need to develop our ability to learn and do things in other ways in order to become more efficient and effective at learning and being productive.

In a nutshell

- People who are productive – who get things done – manage to do so, not just because they have a productive mindset or because they've prioritized their commitments, but also because they draw on their skills, strengths, and qualities.
- Identify your skills and strengths. Think about how each quality has helped you in the past and can continue to help you to be productive; to get things done effectively and efficiently.
- When you're aware of how you learn best – how you take in new ideas and information and acquire new knowledge and skills – you can use it to your advantage and apply your preferred approach to learning to help you be more productive.
- You can find out for yourself what your preferred learning style is by Googling 'Honey and Mumford Learning Style Questionnaire'.

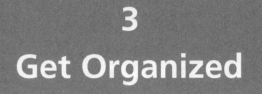

3
Get Organized

There is, of course, always someone who can tell you what you need to do to be more productive and successful. Someone like New Yorker Anthony Pompliano who, one day in June 2018, tweeted a list of nine things that, he said, 'the most successful people' do. Here's his list:

1. Read constantly.
2. Work out daily.
3. Are innately curious.
4. Have laser focus.
5. Believe in themselves.
6. Build incredible teams.
7. Admit they know very little.
8. Constantly work to improve.
9. Demand excellence in everything they do.

He got some amusing responses. Here's one from @TechnicallyRon.

The most successful people I've met:
1. Take good naps.
2. Eat regular meals.
3. Enjoy exercise.
4. Like a good treat.
5. Covered in fur.
6. Aren't actually people.
7. Are golden retrievers.

If you're keen to be more productive, you've probably come across plenty of conflicting advice or hacks that are touted as being the secrets that can set you on the road to success.

But what works for one person may not be the best strategy for someone else. Being productive involves finding your own rhythm and getting things done in a way that works best for *you*; according to *your* circumstances; *your* skills and abilities; and the time, energy, and resources *you* have. Though it can be helpful to get ideas from others who have a knack for getting things done, when it comes to your own productivity, the smartest thing you can do is to learn what works best for *you*.

Productivity Is Personal

'No one is you and that is your power.'

Dave Grohl

You might marvel at how much productive people seem to get done; they appear to be able to fit more into their day than you thought was possible. But what you'll find is that they've set things up to succeed according to *their* skills, strengths, and abilities; *their* resources, interests, commitments, and obligations. And rather than working harder, they're working smarter.

You can do the same.

In Lewis Carroll's *Alice in Wonderland*, Alice has the following conversation with the Cheshire Cat:

> **Alice:** Would you tell me, please, which way I ought to go from here?
> **The Cheshire Cat:** That depends a good deal on where you want to get to.
> **Alice:** I don't much care where.
> **The Cheshire Cat:** Then it doesn't much matter which way you go.
> **Alice:** . . . So long as I get somewhere.
> **The Cheshire Cat:** Oh, you're sure to do that, if only you walk long enough.

When it comes to being productive, if, like Alice, you don't know what, exactly, it is that you're trying to achieve, you could well end up just about anywhere and spend a long time getting there!

Do you want to be more productive at work or study? Perhaps you want to be more productive at home: with housework, decluttering, or decorating. Maybe you'd like to be more productive with a creative activity:

writing a novel, painting or drawing, or learning a new skill – a language or a musical instrument. Maybe you want to achieve more in terms of health and exercise? Perhaps you want to train to run a marathon?

Whatever area or areas of your life that you want to be more productive in, you'll need to have an idea of how much you want to get done and by when.

These goals, for example have no measures or time frames:

1. Get more business.
2. Get fitter.
3. Write a book of short stories.
4. Declutter the house.

In contrast, these goals show how much each person wants to get done and by when.

1. Get 10 new clients in the next year.
2. Be able to run a half marathon by April.
3. Write a book of 10 short stories by the end of the year.
4. Declutter one room in my home every month.

Reality Check

Knowing how much you want to get done and by when can help structure and focus your efforts. But how do you know if what you're aiming for is reasonable and realistic? Realistic goals are achievable, they're based on what's practical – within your capabilities and resources – not based on what you *wish* you could do.

You can begin to see how achievable and realistic your goal is by identifying where you are now in relation to where you want to be.

If, for example, you wanted to get 10 new clients in the next year, you'd need to identify the rate at which you're currently securing new clients. If you want to run a half marathon by April, how far can you run right now? How long until the date of the half marathon? If you want to write a book of 10 short stories in a year, how much do you currently write in any one day or week? And if you want to declutter one room in your home every month, how well have you been able to do that in the past?

Once you've identified the gap between where you're at and where you want to be, you can further identify how realistic and achievable your goal is by breaking it down into steps. Ten new clients, for example, averages out at one new client every five weeks. Is that realistic?

Top Tip

When you consider a goal, also consider a half-size version. Mentally put your original version and the half-size version side by side and ask yourself: which feels the better (more realistic) goal?

Identify Your Options

Next, think about and identify your options: the different possible ways you could work towards your goal.

If, for example, you wanted to write a novel, in order to find the time you might see that you have two options: you could either give up your fulltime job, write in the day, and do a bar job in the evenings and weekends; or you could keep your job, get up early, write for an hour or two before work, and write in the evenings and weekends.

What are the possibilities? Identify all the different means and methods you could use to reach your goal. What skills, strengths, and resources do you have that could help you? (Look back at Chapter 2.) Do you need further information, advice or help? Who could help you? There's more than one way to do things. By identifying a Plan A and a Plan B you can adjust your approach if one strategy isn't working.

Once you're clear about what it is you want to get done, have a realistic idea of how much and by when, and have identified your options and which option you'll take, the next thing to do is to plan how and when you'll do it.

Write It Down

Start by writing down what there is to do. Whether it's your work or home life or both, think of everything you've got going on in a typical day and week. Write it down. And if it's one specific project that you want to focus on – decorating or renovating your home, for example, starting your own business or increasing the number of clients you have – write down everything involved in that project or aspect of your life. Don't worry about writing things down in any order. Just empty your mind of all the things you can think of that you want to do, have to do, and need to do.

Once you've got everything written down, you've got yourself a 'to-do' list.

Unfortunately, though, what often happens is that you get so overwhelmed seeing everything on your list you just don't know where to start. You feel daunted, disillusioned, and discouraged. Seeing what you 'should' get done and 'ought' to do, what you didn't get done, and what you've yet to do, only makes you feel like you're not doing enough. (You *are* doing enough; you're just not doing it efficiently!)

Writing a list is a good start. But it's just one step on the road to getting things done.

Plan And Prioritize

You may have been told this before – but no matter how many times you hear it, it's still true: you need to plan and prioritize. Planning means clearly identifying how and when you will do each task or step of a task.

Prioritizing involves identifying the order for dealing with tasks according to their relative importance.

But although the need to plan and prioritize might be an obvious truth, remember that what's also true is that, as with all other aspects of being productive, you need to plan and prioritize according to *your* circumstances, *your* skills and abilities, and the time, energy, and resources *you* have.

So, where to start? What to do first? What's important? What's not important? What's a priority?

No doubt there are things you don't want to do but need to do; and things you want to do *and* need to do.

There are probably things you want to do but actually don't need to do. And there are things you don't want to do and don't need to do. Some things are urgent. Some things are important. And some things are urgent *and* important.

Urgent And Important

US President Dwight D. Eisenhower once said: 'What's important is seldom urgent and what's urgent is seldom important.' What did he mean by this? Simply that by attending to what's important, things rarely become urgent.

When things become urgent, they also become important; they become urgent *and* important tasks.

Urgent and important tasks are the things that shout 'Do it now'! So, often, they're the things you have to do because you've left them to the last minute and there will be consequences if you don't deal with them immediately. Typically, urgent important tasks are the things with deadlines: essays and reports, job and visa applications, tax returns, passport and insurance renewals. Getting the car serviced or the MOT done and getting dinner on the table.

If you spend too much time on urgent things, it's like you're chasing cows instead of building fences; you don't have much time to spend on the important things, the tasks that really could make a difference and help you avoid the urgent things becoming an issue.

By spending time identifying and planning the important things, you can prevent problems that, if not dealt with now, may become urgent tasks – even crises – in future. It's not just the big projects, it can be the most straightforward, everyday things too. Things like the time spent queuing in your lunch hour for a stamp for the card for your grandmother's 90th birthday tomorrow. Or urgent dental work that you have to get done because you didn't bother going for a check-up for ages. Now you're in pain and have to take time off to get your teeth fixed. Or the time and money spent on getting the boiler fixed because you didn't get it serviced. Or, as used to happen to me when my children were of school age, the stressful time I spent in a crowded shoe shop the week before term started again. All these things are important, but because they got put off, they became urgent!

Of course, it's not always easy to get motivated to do something if there's no deadline looming over your head. Even though they might, in the long run, be important, those tasks aren't pressing, so it's easy to keep them on the back burner and tell yourself that you *will* get to those things at some point. You can find out ways to overcome procrastination in Chapter 4, but in the meantime, know that if you don't prioritize and plan the important things you'll always be chasing cows instead of building fences.

When you spend time planning and working on important – but not urgent – tasks, you can prevent and eliminate many of the crises and problems that come with the urgent tasks. You'll feel more in control and therefore be able to be more productive.

So, what's important?

You might have heard of Pareto's Principle: the 80/20 law. The 80/20 law – the law of the vital few – refers to the observation that most things in life are not distributed evenly. The Pareto Principle can be applied to being productive in a couple of ways. It could be, for example, that 80% of your efforts are only achieving 20% of what you want to get done. Looking at it another way, if you have a list of ten things do, only two of those tasks – 20% – will be important, but you busy yourself instead with the eight least important – the 80% that contributes very little to you getting things done.

So, what can you do in order to apply the 80/20 rule in a way that will get things done effectively and efficiently? You can identify what, on your list, is and isn't important. Two things are important: first, what you *have* to get done – your obligations and commitments; second – what you *want* to get done – the things you want to be productive with.

Once you've identified what's important – what you want to achieve – look at your to-do list and decide which tasks help you make progress on meaningful work. Ask yourself: 'Is this task in the top 20% – what's important – or in the bottom 80%?'

Plan

> 'Planning's not just sensible, it's the rope that guides you through the wilderness.'
>
> Emma Donoghue

A study by professors Veronika Brandstätter and Peter Gollwitzer published in 1997 in the *Journal of Personality and Social Psychology* shows that *scheduling* what needs doing makes it much more likely that things will get done. Brandstätter and Gollwitzer found that 'difficult goal intentions were completed about three times more often when participants had furnished them with implementation intentions'.

What that means in plain English is that you're more likely to do something if you identify when, exactly, you're going to do it.

You've probably experienced something being more likely to happen when you schedule it in your social life. You bump into someone you haven't seen for a while and, after a brief chat, as you're about to go your separate ways, you say to each other 'we must get together some time'. Most likely, nothing happens. If though, right there and then, you actually set a date and a time to meet up in the future, it's much more likely that you will meet up.

Quite simply, that which is scheduled actually gets done.

So, what to schedule: what to do and when to do it? Look at your list. You might want to schedule the important things on your list first or you might want to knock out a bunch of small tasks first.

The American writer Mark Twain suggested that 'If it's your job to eat a frog, it's best to do it first thing in the morning. And if it's your job to eat two frogs, it's best to eat the biggest one first.' The frog is that one thing you have on your to-do list that you can't face doing and that you're most likely to put off. 'Eating the frog' means you just do it. The idea is that once the frog is eaten – once the biggest, ugliest, hardest task is done – everything else you plan on doing the rest of the day will be easy.

There's a couple of reasons why this advice might not be right for you. To begin with, the biggest task might be so daunting and unappealing that the prospect of dealing with it puts you off from doing anything useful at all. You can't even face a small frog! Perhaps you'd prefer to start your day with some easy things to do. If you're able to knock off several easy tasks first – one right after another – you may well feel ready to tackle the harder tasks.

Often, the main hurdle is just getting started. What could be called 'constructive procrastination' eases this difficulty because working on easy tasks requires less mental or physical commitment than tackling difficult tasks first. So, if for you one of the challenges to productivity is simply getting going, it makes sense to save the difficult tasks for when you're in more of a groove.

In fact, small measures of progress can help to kickstart momentum and make it more likely that you will move on to the harder tasks. If you can successfully get a few relatively unimportant things done, your day then develops a slant of productivity; of efficiency and effectiveness. You might also find that getting some urgent tasks done and off your to-do list frees you to think clearly about the bigger stuff.

Getting started with the easy stuff, getting some quick wins and feeling good about your progress, means it's easier to build momentum. In contrast, 'eating the frog' – feeling that you 'should' start with the difficult tasks that you don't want to do – means that you set yourself up for a stressful start. Lots of people aren't at their best at the beginning of the day. Like them, you might need to ease into the workday; do some mundane chores first. If this is you, resolving to do your most difficult tasks first would be a mistake.

It might be that when you start with the hardest tasks first, you drain physical and mental energy. Then you're flagging but still looking at a handful of small jobs on your to-do list. Now what could've been easy becomes hard!

Optimize Your Time

For many people, maximum productivity hours *do* occur in the morning, but this isn't true for everyone.

It all very much depends on your optimum times of day; the times in the day when your physical and mental energy and concentration levels are at their best; when you have the most physical and mental energy for different types of tasks.

Some tasks – for example, researching, reading, writing bids and reports, or filling in forms – need all your focus and concentration. However, it's not a good use of time and energy if you try to do these things at a time of day when you're not at your best. Attempt a task when you're unable to concentrate and the law of diminishing returns kicks in: each minute of effort produces fewer and fewer results. It's difficult to be focused and engaged and you're more likely to be easily distracted.

On the other hand, getting things done at your *most* optimum time of day will take less effort and energy because it's easier for you to focus and concentrate on what's happening and what needs doing.

Think about whether you're a morning, afternoon, or evening person. If you're not sure, try out different times of day and different amounts of time on various activities to see when you have the most mental and physical energy.

Identify what sort of jobs or activities you can only spend a short time on. Are you easily bored or distracted by some tasks? Probably best to plan to do them when your ability to focus is at its highest: at your optimum time of day.

Top Tip

Work out what's the optimum amount of time you can focus on different tasks and activities. It may be that you're best doing things in short bursts rather than one big stretch. So, that might mean that three

---

> sessions of 20 minutes' focused attention could be better than one long 60-minute slog. Experiment. Try the 'short bursts' technique and see if it works for you.

Of course, your circumstances may not allow you to choose when you do particular tasks or activities, so you'll have to be flexible and work out the best compromise possible. If your best time of day is in the morning, but you have other commitments that prevent you from using your optimum time for work that needs concentration and focus, if possible negotiate with your manager or colleagues to free up some of your optimum time.

Once you know which hours are less productive for you, you can plan and schedule easy, mundane tasks for those times. And knowing which times of the day are not your most productive can help you stop feeling guilty, because you know it just isn't the best time for you to get work done.

Create Routines

Whether you want to be more productive at work or at home, on a specific project or aspect of your life, what tasks do you do every day? What tasks do you do every week? To be more productive, you need to create some efficient processes for handling those repetitive tasks. You need to create a routine – a set schedule for doing chores, tasks, and all the things you want to do or need to do most often.

The idea of routines may sound regimented, boring, and uninspiring, but they're a key element of being productive. Routines predetermine your schedule, allowing you to use your time efficiently. In fact, routines have several benefits.

Routines Reduce Procrastination And Reduce The Number Of Decisions You Need To Make

When tasks and activities become routine, this reduces the chance that you'll put off doing them. When, for example, you brush your teeth each morning and evening, you hardly think about having to do it; you simply do it. You do it because it's routine; something you do so regularly it has become automatic. The same holds true for other tasks when you make them part of a routine; you don't waste time each day thinking about it and deciding what and when to do something. You just get on with it.

In an interview in 2012, President Obama told the magazine *Vanity Fair* 'You'll see I wear only gray or blue suits. I'm trying to pare down decisions. I don't want to make decisions about what I'm eating or wearing because I have too many other decisions to make.'

It wasn't just what he wore each day that Obama routinized. Important issues requiring a decision from the President were submitted in writing (known as 'decision memos') with three check-boxes at the bottom: 'agree', 'disagree', and 'let's discuss'. 'You need,' he said in the interview, 'to focus your decision-making energy. You need to routinize yourself.'

Routines Reduce Stress

If you always keep your things in the same place, you don't waste time and energy looking for them. If, for example, you always keep your car and house keys in the same place, you avoid the stress of having to find them because you always know where they are. It's the same principle for the things you need to do: if they're part of a routine you don't get stressed thinking about when you can do them; when you can fit them in. You already know that you have a set time to do them. And, if you've made certain tasks part of your routine, there's no risk of forgetting them; you know that they'll always get done.

Routines Provide Familiarity And Stability

When a task or set of tasks are routine, they become something you know you can do well. When other things are uncertain or out of control, routines provide an anchor of predictability and stability.

Routines Create Structure And Flow So You Become More Effective and Efficient

Routines provide structure, and also a logical sequence to your day and your week. A routine allows you to experience a flow to your day; things proceed continuously and smoothly. When you've completed one thing, you know what's next to do and you become more efficient as a result. Furthermore, because a task is routine, you become better at doing it *because* you do it regularly.

'A good daily routine is a way of tackling whatever obstacles you have in your daily life', says journalist and author Mason Currey. 'It's taking stock of your commitments, temperament and goals, and devising a scheme that suits your project, your quirks and your personality.'

A few years ago, as a result of a particularly unproductive afternoon, Mason – author of dailyroutines .typepad.com (now a book: *Daily Rituals: How Artists Work*) – began looking on the internet for information about other writers' working schedules. He came across interviews, biographies, obituaries, and anecdotes about the working lives of a range of creatives – Freud, Beethoven, and Georgia O'Keeffe among others – and saw that a feature of their days and weeks was a set routine. Although the subjects of his research had structured their days with a routine to do their work (writers especially have two clear blocks of work, separated by a walk or an activity of some sort), Mason discovered that there is no one daily routine which works and can be recommended for everyone.

Mason writes that routines 'can be a finely calibrated mechanism for taking advantage of a range of limited resources: time (the most limited resource of all) as well as will power, self discipline and optimism. A solid routine fosters a well worn groove for one's mental energies and helps stave off the tyranny of moods.'

In other words, routines can help you minimize or overcome difficulties such as lack of time and self-discipline, distractions and interruptions, and maximize your opportunities to be creative and productive.

Batch Tasks

We each have to work it out for ourselves and devise routines that take into account the tasks we have, our circumstances and abilities, and the time, energy, and resources we have. Start with anything that has to be done at a certain time each day (like doing the school run or taking your lunch break). Then slot in tasks based on when it makes the most sense for you to do them.

Think about when the best time of day is for you to do things. And think about which tasks can be 'batched' together.

The idea behind batching is to identify similar tasks and plan to do them one at a time, in one timeframe.

You can work efficiently on several tasks without losing your flow if the activities require similar mindsets. Because the tasks are similar, they keep your attention and you stay focused.

To discover which tasks you can batch, look at all the things you've written down that you have to do in any one day or week. Now identify the ones that are similar and batch them together. You might, for example, batch all your communications – e-mails, phone calls, and texts – and schedule them at a certain time or times of your day. So, instead of putting 'Call back my sister' or 'Phone the client' on your to-do list, establish a recurring block of time each afternoon to return phone calls, texts, and e-mails.

Are you constantly up and down, scanning or copying things? Make a folder and put things in it throughout the day, if you don't need something right away, so that you don't forget what you wanted to copy but you only do it once, all at one time.

And at home, you might batch together repairs, cleaning, and decluttering tasks for regular set times.

Task Switch

But batching isn't the only way to get lots of things done in a specific amount of time. In fact, 'batching' might not appeal to you *because* it involves doing a run of similar tasks and chores in one time period. You might be someone who prefers a change in the nature of each task. If that's the case, then you'll probably be more productive – more effective and efficient – if you get things done by 'task switching'.

For example, you might not want to follow one meeting with another. You might want to follow a meeting with some time spent at your computer. Or you might not want to spend time writing a report and follow that with a similar task such as filling in an application form. Instead, you could follow the report writing with taking your turn to do the coffee run.

Whatever the tasks, the way to task switch effectively is to work on one task at a time but alternate between them.

In fact, whether you intend to batch tasks or task switch, the approach is the same: identify what, exactly, you're going to be doing; be clear about which tasks you're going to work on and know which task will follow on from the last. Once you're clear about the sequence of tasks and how much time you'll spend on each one, get started. Do one thing at a time. Do it mindfully and focus on it completely. Then move onto the next task or activity. Give that your full attention too. If you start thinking about the other tasks, remind yourself that you've already scheduled it in and pull yourself back to the task in hand.

Top Tip

See for yourself if you work best when following one completed task with a similar related task – batching, or if it helps to alternate completely different tasks – task switching.

But isn't all this batching and task switching just multitasking? No. It's single tasking. And that's the crucial thing: whether you batch tasks or switch tasks, you just focus on *one* thing at a time. Don't try to do two things at once.

Multitasking

Is it, though, possible to multitask: to do two things at the same time? Yes.

If you find it difficult to multitask it's probably because you're trying to do *incompatible* things at the same time. If, for example, you're surfing the web while talking on the phone, or writing an e-mail while trying to watch a film, you're not going to be able to do either of them very well; your concentration isn't completely focused on any of the tasks. Reading at the same time as listening to someone talk is very difficult; they are too similar for your brain to manage both at once.

However, doing a physical task – such as making or mending – with a mental task – such as listening to music or listening to someone talking – is much more doable. So is rehearsing what you want to say in a presentation while you're washing dishes or ironing; and so is watching something on a screen while running on a treadmill.

The key to multitasking is to match tasks that are complementary rather than competitive. Matching tasks with other compatible tasks not only makes multitasking possible, but for some tasks it makes it more productive than single tasking.

Work out for yourself which mental tasks you can do at the same time as you're doing physical tasks and what the best time of day to do this is.

Top Tip

You may find that the easier, repetitive tasks that you regularly do can be best linked to something that's more difficult. For example, you might cook a meal every evening. You might also be learning a language. So, you could link the cooking with the learning. 'If I'm cooking, then I'll listen to a language lesson.'

Batching, task switching, and multitasking: all three approaches can help streamline your day, making more things simpler and more efficient.

Of course, not everything needs to be scheduled or incorporated into a routine and you don't have to stick to it rigidly. Experiment. Have a go at multitasking. See if it's easier to task switch or to batch tasks together. Try out a new routine for a few days or a couple of weeks and see how it works for you. Do you need to adjust things? If something isn't working, change it. Just remain flexible and open to changing how you do things.

Obviously, there will always be urgent tasks that you couldn't have foreseen. You can't always predict or avoid some issues and crises. That's why, just like having savings to deal with unexpected financial issues, it's a good idea to plan for some time in your day and week to handle unexpected issues. Make some space. Don't plan things close together; instead, leave room between activities and tasks. That makes your time more flexible and leaves space in case some things take longer than you planned.

Deadlines

The Second World War leader and US President Dwight D. Eisenhower once said that in preparing for battle it's important to know that: 'Plans are worthless, but planning is everything'. There's wisdom in this paradox. To better understand this, we need to see Eisenhower's comment in full. He says:

'I tell this story to illustrate the truth of the statement I heard long ago in the Army: Plans are worthless, but planning is everything. There is a very great distinction because when you are planning for an emergency you must start with this one thing: the very definition of "emergency" is that it is unexpected, therefore it is not going to happen the way you are planning.'

Eisenhower is acknowledging that the outcomes of a plan do not reflect how things will eventually unfold.

So why plan at all if plans are worthless? He goes on to say: 'So, the first thing you do is to take all the plans off the top shelf and throw them out the window and start once more. But if you haven't been planning you can't start to work, intelligently at least.'

It's true; no matter how much you plan, problems, setbacks, difficulties, and challenges happen. You then have to let go of your plans. And plan again.

Is this what happens when things become urgent? Yes. But the problem is, when things become urgent it's not easy to engage your brain so that you can make fresh plans. When there's too much to do and too little time to do it all it's easy to panic and think 'I'm never going to be able to get this done in time!' You feel anxious, frustrated, and stressed. It's impossible to think clearly. Why is that? It's all down to two specific areas of your brain: the amygdala and the neo cortex.

The neo cortex part of your brain is responsible for thinking, remembering, rationalizing, and reasoning. Focus and attention are primarily an activity of the neo cortex. The problem is, when you become stressed, the amygdala is triggered and it overwhelms the neo cortex. The amygdala in your brain is responsible for your emotions – emotions such as agitation, anxiety, and frustration which, when you're under pressure, can overwhelm your neo cortex and so prevent you from thinking rationally and reasonably.

But some people thrive and rise to the challenge of deadlines. How come? Because they just stay with what's happening now. They're completely focused. They don't allow the amygdala to take over; instead, they engage the neo cortex – the thinking, reasoning part of the brain.

You can do the same. Instead of letting yourself get stressed, recognize that there is only a certain amount of time available to get something done. Accept it. Then, once you've accepted the short amount of time you've got, you can engage the reasoning, thinking part of your brain and can think clearly and deliberately. Approaching a deadline in this way is taking a mindful approach: you simply focus on what you're doing right now, at the present time, instead of getting stressed by filling your mind with what you haven't done and what else you've got to do.

Even when things are urgent, you can still prioritize and plan what needs to be done. Don't, though, wait until you're in the middle of the first step to decide what else needs to be done to get things finished on time. Before you do anything, work out what's important; what tasks will contribute to meeting that deadline.

It's easier to get straight on to the next step if you have already planned what and how you are going to do it. It allows you to maintain a steady pace and keep the pace going. A step-by-step plan allows you to simply work consistently towards what it is you want to achieve; so that at any one point in the hour or the day, you're clear about what you are going to work on.

Then get started. Focus. Decide what the first thing you need to do is. Then do that one thing. Give it your full attention. Once that one thing is done, go on to the next step. Give that your full attention too. Keep your mind focused on one step at a time. Tell yourself, 'This is what I'm going to do next', and then just focus on that one step you're taking.

With this focused step-by-step approach, you can be deliberate and purposeful, not rushed and random. You set yourself up to meet the deadline by achieving small targets along the way and you see yourself moving forward.

No matter how little time you have, though, do try and take some breaks. Breaks give your mind space to digest, mentally process, and assimilate what's happening, what is working and what isn't, and to decide if you need to change anything.

Top Tip

Use deadlines and time limits to your advantage. 'Parkinson's law' states: 'work expands so as to fill the time available for its completion'. So, if you reduce the time you have to complete a task, you

---

force yourself to focus and complete it. Try setting deadlines even when you don't need to. Schedule less time to complete tasks and force your brain to focus.

In a nutshell

- Productivity is personal: it involves finding your own rhythm and getting things done in a way that works best for *you;* according to *your* circumstances; *your* skills and abilities; and the time, energy, and resources *you* have.
- Once you're clear about what you want to get done and have a realistic idea of how much and by when – and have identified which option you'll take – the next thing to do is to plan how and when you'll do it.
- If you don't prioritize and plan the important things you'll always be chasing cows instead of building fences. By spending time identifying and planning the important things, you can prevent problems that, if not dealt with now, may become urgent tasks – even crises – in future.
- Look at your to-do list and decide which tasks help you make progress on meaningful work. Ask yourself: 'Is this task in the top 20% – what's important – or in the bottom 80%?'
- You might need to ease into your day. If so, resolving to do your most difficult tasks first

would be a mistake. Instead, get started with the easy stuff. Getting some quick wins and feeling good about your progress means it's easier to build momentum. Save the difficult tasks for when you're in more of a groove.

- It's not a good use of time and energy if you try to do things at a time of day when you're not at your best. Attempt a task when you're unable to concentrate and the law of diminishing returns kicks in: each minute of effort produces fewer and fewer results. It's difficult to be focused and engaged and you're more likely to be easily distracted.
- On the other hand, getting things done at your most optimum time of day will take less effort and energy because it's easier for you to focus and concentrate on what's happening and what needs doing.
- Identify what sort of jobs or activities you can only spend a short time on. Are you easily bored or distracted by some tasks? Probably best to plan to do them when your ability to focus is at its highest; at your optimum time of day.
- Once you know which hours are less productive for you, you can plan and schedule easy, mundane tasks for those times. And knowing which times of the day are not your most productive can help you stop feeling guilty because you know it just isn't the best time for you to get work done.

- Routines are a key element of being productive. Routines predetermine your schedule: they create structure and flow to your day. Routines can help you minimize or overcome procrastination, indecisiveness, lack of time and self-discipline, distractions and interruptions.
- You can work efficiently on several tasks without losing your flow if the activities require similar mindsets. Because the tasks are similar, they keep your attention and you stay focused. Think about which tasks can be 'batched' together; identify similar tasks and plan to do them one at a time, in one timeframe.
- If you're someone who prefers a change in the nature of each task, then you'll probably be more productive – more effective and efficient – if you get things done by 'task switching'.
- Whether you batch tasks or task switch, the approach is the same: be clear about which tasks you're going to work on and know which task will follow on from the last. Do one thing at a time and focus on it completely. Then move onto the next task or activity. Give that your full attention too. Just focus on one thing at a time. Don't try to do two things at once.
- It is, though, possible to do two things at the same time. The key to multitasking is to match tasks that are complementary rather than competitive.
- Experiment. See if it's easier to task switch or to batch tasks together. Try out a new routine

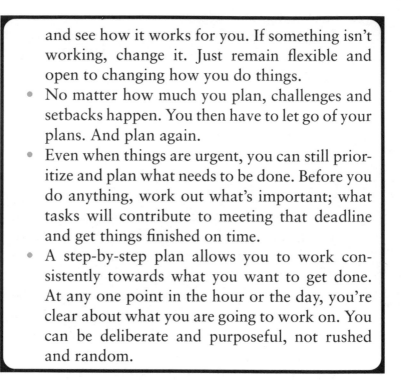

and see how it works for you. If something isn't working, change it. Just remain flexible and open to changing how you do things.

- No matter how much you plan, challenges and setbacks happen. You then have to let go of your plans. And plan again.
- Even when things are urgent, you can still prioritize and plan what needs to be done. Before you do anything, work out what's important; what tasks will contribute to meeting that deadline and get things finished on time.
- A step-by-step plan allows you to work consistently towards what you want to get done. At any one point in the hour or the day, you're clear about what you are going to work on. You can be deliberate and purposeful, not rushed and random.

4
Manage The Difficulties And Setbacks

It's not just deadlines – unexpected or otherwise – that can get in the way of being productive. There will be times when you struggle to get started and find yourself demotivated, off-course, or discouraged. There will be interruptions, delays, hold-ups, and setbacks.

Let's start with getting started. If you're in the habit of putting off getting started on a task or project, you've probably become very good at coming up with other activities that are, all of a sudden, more important or enjoyable.

It's easy to persuade yourself, for example, that filling in your expense claims or finishing writing a report can wait. Right now, cleaning the kitchen is more important. Of course, under normal circumstances, cleaning the kitchen wouldn't be something you'd be in a rush to get started on – but compared with filling in your expense claims, marking those essays, or getting started on writing that report, a bit of cleaning becomes an attractive alternative! Or maybe you've persuaded yourself that you'll get started on that new project once you've answered a few e-mails. Perhaps you've convinced yourself that you really *must;* it's imperative those e-mails get answered right now.

How does this happen? Why is it that despite your good intentions, it's so easy to put things off? A good way to understand it is by imagining that you have two selves: your 'present self' and your 'future self'. When you set goals for yourself, you're making plans for your future self and your future life. And it looks good!

However, while you can have good intentions for your future self, only your present self can do something about them. And when the time comes to actually do something, you're no longer making a choice for your future self. Now you're in the present and you are having to make a decision for your present self.

So, the present self and the future self are in conflict. 'I ought to get started. But do I really have to do this now? Can't it wait till later? I really should do something. But I can't be bothered.'

Your future self wants to have achieved something; but the present self can't make the effort. Why?

Your good intentions come from the rational, reasoning part of your brain – the part that thinks things through and recognizes the benefits of doing something and eventually achieving it. However, in the present moment, it's easy for emotions to take over; feelings of apathy and resentment can undermine your intentions and convince you *not* to do something.

Perhaps, though, you feel overwhelmed by pressure. Putting things off can often be a way of coping with any uncertainty or anxiety you feel about the activity. If what you have to do is something new – an unfamiliar task – you might be unsure about how to do it or be unsure about how much time it will take to complete. Furthermore, if it's not urgent – if the deadline is far off – it's easier to do nothing or to do a familiar task instead.

You tell yourself, for example, that you're too tired or that you don't have enough time or you've got other more important things that need to be done. Or perhaps you realize that your expectations about what you could get done are unrealistic. Maybe you set your sights too high? Perhaps you have unrealistic ideas about what you're capable of or 'should' be doing.

Whatever the reason, you're procrastinating.

Even though you know the benefits of achieving whatever it is you're aiming to do, and that there may be consequences if you don't get going, it's not enough; you can't always rely on long-term rewards and consequences to motivate your present self.

It's only when future consequences become present consequences that you get going. For example, imagine you have an essay or a report to write. You've known about it for weeks and continued to put it off. You feel irritated and guilty, but not enough to do anything about it. But, of course, a few days before the deadline, the future consequences turn into present consequences! You write and complete that report hours before it's due.

Not all procrastination is equal, though. It can – as you will have read in the last chapter – be a form of prioritization; maybe you have to wait till the last minute to get started because the pressure forces you to focus.

So, are you using procrastination effectively or does it get in the way of you being productive?

The thing is, procrastination can be more painful than the actual work. In order to get motivated, you tell yourself that you 'should' do this, you 'ought' to make a start, and you 'must' get going. Your inner critic reprimands you and you give yourself a hard time. But remonstrating with yourself doesn't make you want to get on with it, it just makes you feel guilty, frustrated, and resentful. Bad enough that you keep putting things off, but if you feel guilty about not having met your good intentions, you keep the negative feelings going and you find it even harder to motivate yourself the next time you attempt to get started.

The guilt and anxiety that you feel while procrastinating are often more unpleasant than the effort and energy you have to put in while you're working. The problem is not doing the work, it's starting the work. Imagine how much less guilt, stress, and frustration you would feel if you could somehow just make yourself do the things you don't want to get started on. Not to mention how much more efficient and effective you would be.

We've already seen that one way to make a start on something is to wait until it's urgent and you really *have* to make a start. There is, though, another way to overcome procrastination. It's a way of thinking and doing that will give you the kickstart you need.

Get A Kickstart

If you're like most people, you believe that before you can do anything – in order to get started on something – you need to feel like you want to take action. It's not true. You don't need to feel like doing it.

Waiting until you *really* feel like doing something is a sure-fire way for things *not* to get done. As novelist and prolific writer Stephen King points out: 'Amateurs sit and wait for inspiration, the rest of us just get up and go to work.'

Stop wallowing in guilt and resentment. Accept how you feel. It's normal *not* to feel like it in the beginning. It's normal to feel that you're not 'in the zone'.

Just do it. In times like this, accept your feelings and get on with it. Do the work.

Top Tip

Make use of a mindfulness concept known as 'acceptance and commitment'. When you can't get it together to get started, you ask yourself: 'What do I feel right now?' Deprived? Irritated? Resentful? Instead of fighting these feelings or giving in to them, acknowledge and *accept* them. Then remind yourself of the reasons why you want to do something and *commit* yourself to doing it.

Motivation comes from doing. The fact is, you *will* get into the zone once you actually get started. You just need to be prepared to move through that reluctant feeling on your way to achieving what you want to get done. That's what productive people do. They often don't feel like getting started either.

Carla works three days a week as a freelance copy editor. She says: 'I enjoy my work but I find it really hard to get started in the mornings and after lunch. What gets me going though, isn't the fact that I have strong willpower (I don't) it's because I know that "feeling like it" rarely comes before taking action.'

'I find that if I just sit down at my computer, although I don't feel like it initially, I make a start and before I know it I'm absorbed in what I'm doing and I'm just getting on with it. So that's what gets me started – knowing that I will feel like it if I just make that big but short effort to get started.'

This approach is effective because of one simple reason: the physics of real life. As Sir Isaac Newton discovered, objects at rest tend to stay at rest. But objects in motion tend to stay in motion. This is just as true for humans as it is for falling apples! When you generate the physical motions, they in turn trigger the thoughts – the positive mindset – which correspond to that physical action.

Act 'As If'

If you're waiting until you feel ready – until you really feel like it – before you take action, you may find that acting 'as if' will help. Acting 'as if' is a way to create motivation to do something even though you may not feel like doing it. It simply requires you to make a start on something 'as if' you're only going to spend a short amount of time – five minutes, ten minutes, or half an hour – on it. The momentum takes over and you find yourself easily carrying on with whatever it is you intended to do. All it takes is a little effort at the start.

Whatever it is that you need to make a start on, make a deal with yourself: tell yourself you'll do it for just five minutes. Instead of putting things off; instead of trying to, for example, answer all those e-mails or sort through all that paperwork or arrange the whole trip or event, tell yourself you'll do it for just five minutes. Start doing something immediately, without thinking and giving your mind time to come up with excuses. You may well find that once you get going, you end up continuing well past the five-minute mark you decided on. If even the smallest task seems too hard, tell yourself you're just going to do five minutes right now.

Once you start doing it, it's easier to continue doing it. Take action and things will flow from there. That's why it is important to have a plan for the steps you need to take; it's easier if you're clear about what you're going to do first and what step will come next.

Decide what is the one thing you can do, then do that one thing. Give it your full attention. Answer that one e-mail. Make that first phone call. Google the information you need. Start filling in that form. Just clear out one drawer. Do one sit up. Put just one thing on eBay. Just read the instructions. Paint one wall. Make that one appointment. Write the first paragraph. You'll find that once you get started, you can keep going.

After a short time, the positive feelings which you would like from doing that activity start to emerge naturally. It's a positive feedback loop – acting 'as if' influences further thoughts and actions. Don't wait until you feel like it to take action. Get going and your thoughts and feelings will change. The momentum takes over and you'll find yourself easily carrying on with whatever it is you intended to do. All it takes is a little effort at the start.

Remember: the guilt and anxiety that you feel while procrastinating are often worse than the effort and energy you have to put in while you're working. The problem is not doing the work, it's starting the work. So just get started!

Make It Even Easier

As well as acting 'as if', there are other ways you can make it easier for yourself to get started. The American writer Ernest Hemingway said 'I always worked until I had something done and I always stopped when I knew what was going to happen next. That way I could be sure of going on the next day.'

Whatever it is you want to do, spend a minute or two setting it up so that it's easier to go forward than to do nothing. Want to go for a swim or a run each morning but can't get your act together? Put your swimming costume or running gear on before you get properly dressed. That way you're far more likely to make a start.

'If ... Then ...'

Trying an 'if ... then ...' approach is another way to make it easier to do something; to make it more likely that you will do something than not. You simply connect what you need or have to do with an already established habit. *If*, for example, you already take the rubbish out each night, *then* water your plants at the same time. You link something you want to do with something you already do – an already established habit.

Watering the plants when you take the rubbish out is, of course, task batching (as explained in Chapter 3). An 'if … then …' approach can also be done with things that can be multitasked. For example, you might cook a meal every evening. You might also be learning a foreign language. So, you could link the cooking with the learning. '*If* I'm cooking, *then* I'll listen to a language lesson.'

And finally, another way to use the 'if … then …' strategy is to link doing something with a reward for doing it. '*If* I answer all these e-mails *then* I'll have a coffee/sit out in the sunshine/go for a run/watch an episode of the box set I'm currently watching.'

Make A Decision

What, though, if the reason that you can't get started is because you can't decide between one course of action and another? Suppose, for example, you still haven't got started on decorating a room because you can't decide on what colours you want. And you can't decide whether to wallpaper or paint the walls. You spend ages agonizing over the pros and cons of each option: you overthink the situation.

Whether it's decorating a room or any other task, you're not confident that you'll definitely be making the 'right' choice and the 'best' decision. You're worried about the consequences of a 'wrong' decision. In fact, sometimes you're so undecided you make no decision. And then nothing gets done. How *do* you make the right choice? How do you know that what you choose will work out and, if it doesn't, that you won't regret not making a different decision? Quite simply, you don't, can't, and won't. You can never know for sure when you make a decision that it's going to turn out well.

In any one situation, identify what exactly is important and what exactly you're hoping to achieve. Trust your intuition, too. When you do feel strongly that a particular path or choice is the right one, know that it's because your decision is in line with your aims.

Do make a well-informed decision but know that the pursuit of more information can be a way of putting off a choice. Don't wait until conditions are perfect, get started now. If new information comes to light after you have made your decision, you can alter your course then.

Still not sure? Have courage. Accept uncertainty; make a choice despite possible unknowns. Know there is no 'right' or 'wrong' decision. When you're finding it difficult to make a decision, for each option ask yourself: 'What's the worst that can happen? How might I deal with that?' Have a back-up plan. Know that you can make a choice and if things don't work out you will already have thought of what to do to manage what happens.

Persistence, Self-Discipline, and Willpower

So, just find a way to get started and things will keep rolling along. Is it that simple? Well, no. There'll still be times when you struggle; when you'll find yourself off-course, bored, frustrated, and discouraged. You get started, you're determined to make some headway, but you come across some problems and you start flagging. You give up or give in. You've lost both your will and your power! How does this happen?

Remember: your good intentions come from the rational, reasoning part of your brain – the part that thinks through what's good for you. When things get difficult, feelings of deprivation and frustration can undermine your intentions and convince you that it's easier to give in and let go. But as someone once said, 'You didn't come this far to only come this far'. And, fortunately, there are a number of things you can do that will help you persist; to keep going even when you don't feel like carrying on any more.

'Nothing in the world can take the place of Persistence. Talent will not; nothing is more common than unsuccessful men with talent. Genius will not; unrewarded genius is almost a proverb. Education will not; the world is full of educated derelicts. Persistence and determination alone are omnipotent. The slogan "Press On" has solved and always will solve the problems of the human race.'
Calvin Coolidge (30th president of the United States)

Persistence needs a degree of willpower. Willpower is the ability to do what you intended to do even when you don't feel like it. Together with self-control, willpower gives you the ability to keep focused and achieve whatever it is you want to get done. But if it helps you fulfil your good intentions, why, for so many of us, is it so difficult to come by? Because, according to many studies, we all have a limited amount of willpower and it's easily used up.

When you have to use willpower and self-control in one situation, there's less willpower available to you for other situations, even if those situations are totally different from each other. Spend an hour (reluctantly) putting together a presentation, and even though you intended to write your Christmas cards or empty the dishwasher, your brain doesn't have enough energy left to motivate you. You've used up your willpower and fallen victim to 'can't power'.

In a number of studies over recent years, Florida State University's Dr Roy Baumeister and colleagues have discovered that making decisions and choices, taking initiatives, and suppressing impulses all seem to draw on the same well of mental energy. They found that straight after accomplishing a task that required them to use their willpower, people are far more likely to struggle with other willpower-related tasks.

Baumeister and colleagues all come to the same conclusion: self-control and willpower can be used up.

Spend the afternoon filling out your passport renewal form, for example, and your brain doesn't have enough energy left to complete that job application; it's too tired to motivate you. Your resolve goes out the window and you put the job application to one side.

But although you may have limited willpower and self-discipline, it can be increased and strengthened. By working on small tasks that you are reluctant to do, you can gain inner strength and develop the ability to overcome your mind's resistance. You can actually train your mind to obey you!

Which of the things on the list below would you rather not do?

- Load the dishwasher or wash the dishes immediately after every meal.
- Make your bed every morning.
- If you're only going up a couple of floors, walk up the stairs rather than taking the lift.
- Get off the tube or bus one stop earlier or park your car 10 minutes from your destination and walk the rest of the way.
- Go for a 10-minute walk every lunchtime.
- Do a small chore that someone else in your home or workplace does, for them: load the dishwasher or change the ink cartridge, for example.

Try doing just one small thing you don't like doing every day for two weeks. Get it done no matter what. Then, when you've completed it, be aware of how you feel for having achieved it. You'll find that when you're able to make yourself do even the smallest things you don't feel like doing, you'll feel more in control and pleased with yourself. This can lead to more positive thinking; for example, 'I can make myself walk up the stairs instead of taking the lift every day, that means I can also …'.

Developing your willpower helps you to stick to your good intentions, it can help you override the thoughts and behaviour that sabotage those intentions.

Top Tip

Talk to yourself. When it comes to motivating yourself, research shows that in a variety of situations, if you address yourself by your own name, your chances of doing well can increase significantly. It might seem weird, but it can focus your thinking and motivate you. Rather than telling yourself, for example, 'Come on. You can do this', address yourself using your name: 'Joe, come on. You can do this.' By using your own name you're distancing yourself from your self. It would appear that this psychological distance encourages self-control, allowing you to think clearly and perform more competently.

Make It Enjoyable

- Whatever it is that you know you might struggle persisting with, before you get started, think of something you'll reward yourself with each hour or every few hours. This in itself sets up something to work towards – a goal. For some tasks, just taking a break and having a cup of tea or coffee might be the reward. For more demanding tasks, you may want to reward yourself by doing something even more enjoyable. Decide for yourself what that can be.

- Think about how you can make the task more enjoyable. Go through your personal finances while listening to calming music. Do it in a different environment. Take your laptop to a cafe, garden, or park and do your work from there. If you've got a tight deadline, have a second cappuccino to provide a boost. If you're working at night, have a glass of wine. Make it easy on yourself!

- Do it with someone else. Things that are difficult to find the enthusiasm to do are especially tedious when doing them alone. So, invite friends over to paint your room and then cook everyone a simple meal or order a curry or pizza. Whatever it is, partner up and get it done!

- Remind yourself why you're doing this. Remind yourself of the good reasons – the benefits – for achieving what it is you want to achieve. Instead of thinking about how hard something is, think about what you will get out of it. For example, rather than thinking about how you can't be bothered, focus on how good you'll feel when you're done.

Avoid Distractions

Even if you might not feel like making a start and getting on with something, there *are* things you can do to make it easier.

A study carried out in 2013 by Wilhelm Hofmann at the University of Chicago suggested that instead of constantly denying themselves, people who appear to have strong willpower and self-discipline are less likely to put themselves in situations that might tempt them in the first place. They 'avoid problematic desires and conflict', says the study's co-author Professor Kathleen Vohs.

You can do the same.

As well as using strategies like 'acting as if' and 'if … then …' to help make it more likely that you'll get going and keep going with something, you can also avoid 'problematic desires and conflict'. You can remove temptations and distractions.

A distraction is anything that diverts your attention, anything that you *allow* yourself to be sidetracked by. Something is only a distraction if you pay attention to it. It can be a pleasant diversion and can either come from yourself – something you're attracted to – or can come as an interruption from someone else. Distractions often mean a lot of energy and effort are needed to get you back to your main task. But distractions *are* in your control.

Only you know what they are and only you can avoid, manage, or minimize them. If it's your phone or e-mails that distract you, turn them off. If you get 20 e-mails and texts a day, this means 20 distractions to your day. Stop reading every e-mail as it arrives. Switch off instant alerts and, instead, choose a specific time when you will check your inbox. Here are some more suggestions:

Remember the adage 'out of sight, out of mind'. It's true; something can't distract you if it's not there or you're not there. Go somewhere where you're not distracted by other people or put headphones on and listen to music to stay focused.

Anticipate your needs before you do something that requires your full attention. Whether you'll need particular information, resources, or just something to drink, get what you need and you'll be less likely to get drawn away from what you intended to focus on.

Train yourself. Practise focus and engagement by turning off all distractions and committing your attention to a single task for a short amount of time (maybe 15 or 30 minutes?) and then work up to longer periods of time.

Keep a list. In what's known in psychology as the 'Zeigarnik effect', uncompleted tasks typically keep popping back into your mind. If, however, you've made a list, whenever thoughts about other work pop into your head, you can remind yourself that you won't forget them because they're on your list. Then pull yourself back to refocus on what you're doing right now.

Do it later. If you feel tempted by a distraction, tell yourself that you will get to it in your break. But not sooner.

Any time you realize you've allowed yourself to be distracted, don't berate yourself, just return to what you were doing. Tell yourself: 'I know I lost focus, but now I'm going to continue with what I'm doing.'

'If you want to fly, you have to give up the things that weigh you down.'

Toni Morison

Do what you can to avoid the situation presenting itself; make the things you struggle to ignore less available and you'll be in a much stronger position. This will minimize the number of times you have to draw on your willpower and self-discipline. It will also save your mental strength for when you really need it.

Plan For Difficulties, Delays, And Setbacks

No matter what you do to avoid distractions and make it easier to persist, you can't control everything; life will always have something unexpected to throw your way. Things happen: the weather changes, a road is closed, someone you were relying on drops out, you get ill or sustain an injury, or it costs more money than you expected.

When there are setbacks and difficulties, looking to lay blame or making excuses about your predicament rarely, if ever, helps the situation. Instead, you need to refocus your attention on what you can do that could help you move forward. If you really want to achieve something, there's usually a way. And, most likely, there's more than one way. As someone once said: 'If plan A doesn't work, the alphabet has 25 more letters.'

Right from when you start planning a task or project you can anticipate potential problems and possible solutions. For each step, think about what could go wrong. What's the worst that could happen? What, for example, will you do if you run out of time, money, or the ability to do something?

Thinking like this is not designed to discourage you and put you off doing something. Quite the opposite. It's making it more likely you'll be successful. How come? Because you've anticipated the potential problems and you've already thought through how you would deal with them. You've already thought about who could help and what support, advice, finances, or resources you could draw on.

Know that when you let go of what you can't control and look at what you can control, you take a step towards getting back on track.

As well as planning for some of the major problems that could crop up, you can plan for the more minor delays that can slow your progress. Meetings get cancelled. People run late. Wi-fi stops working. Things break down and need to be fixed.

From client meetings to dentist appointments, in any one day or week there's usually someone or something keeping you waiting. And if you're a parent of children or young teenagers, waiting times may be a normal part of your life with your child's football practice, swimming lessons, music lessons, etc.

Waiting time can be the most frustrating time if you let it become so. With just a bit of planning, though, you can turn waiting time into productive time. Instead of getting wound up and annoyed with waiting times or when small delays occur, take advantage of them. If you can use these short periods to get small things done, not only will you achieve more but you'll also feel you have some semblance of control.

Make a list of the things you could do to use this time effectively. It could include some of these things:

- Return e-mails and phone calls.
- Learn a computer shortcut.
- Learn how to use functions on your phone that you aren't familiar with, organize your e-mail or photos into folders, or look for new and interesting apps. Learn how to take better photos on your phone. YouTube has plenty of instructional videos.
- Learn a new skill, either for your professional or personal life. Whatever you're interested in, chances are there's an online learning opportunity available. www.duolingo.com, for example, has excellent free courses in French, Spanish, Italian, plus 34 other languages. Whether you're a beginner or already quite proficient in a language, you can

spend as little as two minutes on a lesson or as much as a couple of hours each time.

- Listen to music. Listen to a podcast. Watch a TED talk (www.ted.com).
- Review and plan the rest of your day, tomorrow, or the rest of the week.
- Organize folders on your computer, review and delete e-mails, texts. Edit photos from your phone.
- Plan Christmas or birthday presents.
- Empty the dishwasher.
- Write a food shopping list.
- Make a list of household things that need to be done, cleaned, or repaired.

It's really not that hard to make good use of your time. Have a list of small, easy tasks you can do and do something from that list whenever minor delays and hold-ups occur. You can also draw on this list of small jobs if you need to start your day with easy tasks that help you get into the swing of things.

Of course, you don't have to do anything productive at all. You could use this time to take a break, go for a walk, read a book, play a game, watch something on a screen, do a crossword puzzle or sudoku.

In a nutshell

- Putting things off – procrastinating – can often be a way of coping with any uncertainty or anxiety you feel about the activity. If it's not

---

urgent – if the deadline is far off – it's easier to do nothing or to do something else instead.

- The guilt and anxiety that you feel while procrastinating are often worse than the effort and energy you have to put in while you're working. The problem is not doing the work, it's starting the work.

- Waiting until you really feel like doing something is a sure-fire way for things not to get done. It's normal not to feel like it in the beginning. You don't need to feel like doing it. Just do it. Accept your reluctance and just get on with it. Do the work.

- Motivation comes from doing. The fact is, you will get into the zone once you actually get started. You just need to be prepared to move through that reluctant feeling on your way to achieving what you want.

- Act 'as if'; 'as if' you really want to do it. Tell yourself you'll do it for just five minutes. Once you start doing it, if you know what steps will come next, it's easier to continue doing it.

- 'If … then …' is another way to make it more likely that you will do something. Link something you want to do to something you already do; an already established habit. Or connect a task you're reluctant to do with something you do like doing.

- What if the reason that you can't get started is because you can't decide between one course of action and another? Make a well-informed decision but know that the pursuit of more information can be a way of putting off a choice. Don't wait until conditions are perfect, get started now. If new information comes to light after you have made your decision, you can alter your course then.

- To keep going and achieve whatever it is you want to get done, you'll need to be persistent and you'll need a degree of willpower and self-control.

- Although willpower and self-discipline are finite, they can be increased and strengthened. By working on small tasks that you are reluctant to do, you can gain inner strength and develop the ability to overcome your mind's resistance.

- Make it easier to keep going. Before you get started, think about how you can make the task more enjoyable. Think of something you'll reward yourself with each hour or every few hours. Share the load; do it with someone else.

- Something is only a distraction if you pay attention to it. Distractions are in your control. Make the things you struggle to ignore less available. This will minimize the number of times that you have to draw on your willpower and self-discipline. It will also save your mental strength for when you really need it.

- When there are setbacks and difficulties, you need to refocus your attention on what you can do that could help you move forward. If you really want to achieve something, there's usually a way. And, most likely, there's more than one way.

- Right from when you start planning a task or project you can anticipate potential problems and possible solutions. For each step, think about what could go wrong. What will you do?
- Know that when you let go of what you can't control and look at what you can control, you take a step towards getting back on track.
- As well as planning for some of the major problems that could crop up, you can plan for the more minor delays that can slow your progress.
- Turn waiting time into productive time. Have a list of small, easy tasks you can do and do something from that list whenever minor delays and hold-ups occur. Not only will you get more things done, but you'll also feel you have some semblance of control.

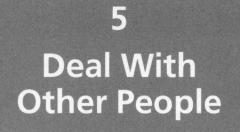

5
Deal With
Other People

When it comes to being productive, to some extent other people can be a help or a hindrance; they can either contribute towards you getting things done or they can create problems and make things difficult. The trick is to manage the hindrances and make use of the help.

Do you ask for help when you don't know how to do something or you can't cope with what needs doing? Or do you just struggle through it? Whether at work or at home, trying to do everything can leave you stressed and overwhelmed. Maybe, though, you don't want anyone to see that you're struggling; rather than look like you're incompetent, you want people to think that you know what you're doing, that you're coping and in control. Perhaps you think asking for help is a sign of weakness; that by asking for help you're admitting that you're inadequate in some way, that you lack the knowledge, skill, or experience to do something yourself.

Or, it could be that, like the participants in a series of studies in 2008, you assume that if you ask others for help they'll say no. In one of the studies, Professor Frank Flynn at Stanford Graduate School of Business and Vanessa Lake at Columbia University looked at people's estimation of how likely others were to help them out. They asked participants in the study to ask other people to do something for them: to fill in a questionnaire, to lend their mobile phone, or to show them how to get to the university campus gym (for which the students would need to walk two blocks out of their way). The study found that participants underestimated by 50% the number of people who would agree to help them.

It appears, then, that other people are more willing to help than you might think. But if you don't ask, the answer is already no!

Productive people often ask others for help, not only because they're secure enough to admit they're struggling and need help, but also because they know that trying to do everything themselves is not always the best use of their time, skills, or energy. They know that trying to cope on their own can leave them feeling overwhelmed and stressed. And then they can't do *anything* properly!

While there's definitely something to be said for trying to work things out and resolve an issue yourself first, struggling for hours or days before finally getting help is almost never productive. Why struggle with some technological nightmare, for example, when you know a friend or colleague who could easily sort it for you? And why try to fit in a supermarket shop in your lunch hour when you could have asked someone else you live with to pick up some bits and pieces on their way home?

Asking for help doesn't mean you're inadequate, it simply means you need support and assistance with something specific for a specific amount of time.

Don't use up your time and energy doing tasks that others may have the time and/or ability to do! Get things done properly and more easily; find someone who's got the time or is good at what you need to learn or get done and then ask for their help and guidance. Know that asking for some help with understanding something at work, for example, acknowledges the other person's knowledge and abilities. And also be aware that if the problem is an aspect of a team project or social event, you are letting other people down by *not* seeking help; you're not the only one affected if you refuse to seek support!

Asking for help – or simply delegating some tasks and chores – gives you more time to focus on what's most important, useful, or necessary. It can free you up to focus on what you – and maybe only you – can do well.

So, get help when you need it. If you need others to help, to give ideas, to solve problems with you, don't hesitate to draw them in. If you're in a position of authority, you can delegate; give a particular job, task, or duty to someone else so that they do it for you. Otherwise, you simply ask. Here's how:

Know what, exactly, you want help with and what needs doing. The clearer you are about what you want help with, the better you can explain it to someone else. People who successfully delegate and get help are clear about what they want. They make it easy for others to understand what needs doing, how, and by when.

Ask directly. One of Flynn and Lake's studies found that those asking for help believed it was more likely they would receive it if they were indirect about it, rather than asking directly. But, actually, the other people said they were much more likely to give assistance if they *were* asked directly; they said that a direct request was not easy to turn down!

So, be direct. Don't drop hints. Don't say 'God this is difficult'. Or 'I've got so much to do'. Don't waffle or apologize for needing help. Don't say 'I know you're really busy, so only if you have time/only if you want to …'. Instead, just tell the other person what you're trying to achieve and what you'd like them to do. Simply say, 'I need help with … Would you be able to … show me/do it for me/get it for me …?' This way, the person is clear about what, how, and when to help you.

Make it easy for someone to help you. Ask the right person for their help – someone who has the ability, knowledge, or time. Unless you've got plenty of time to show someone or train them to do something that's unfamiliar to them, make sure that what you ask them to do matches their skills and ability.

However, don't always assume you know what other people can do. Even if those you ask can't help you directly, they might know someone who can help, they might have some ideas or solutions or some other information that would help you. Until you ask, you don't know who or what other people know or can do!

Delegate, don't dump. Sometimes, what passes for delegation, for the other person feels like they've been dumped on; that you've just offloaded work onto them without any thought or consideration for their situation. Does the other person actually have time to take on more work? Will delegating a job to them mean they will need to reshuffle their current commitments? If so, what do they think and how do they feel about that? What are their concerns? Ask them. Include people in the delegation process. If possible, be flexible. Offer options and negotiate.

Follow-up. If you ask someone to do something for you, be clear about what needs doing but let them determine the process. Be available to answer questions but don't micromanage; focus on the end result rather than detailing exactly how the work should be done. Your way is not necessarily the only or even the best way! Let people do things their own way.

Say thank you. Finally, of course, make sure you express your appreciation; the other person will know that their efforts have been acknowledged and they will be more likely to help out next time!

Top Tip

Review your workload regularly. Is there one task that always ends up at the bottom of the pile? If you find you're avoiding it, can somebody else do it? Over the next couple of weeks, write down all the tasks and activities your job involves and then categorize them according to your level of skill and enjoyment. Then, as far as possible, spend your time and energy focusing on your skills and strengths, and delegate everything else.

Manage Interruptions

As much as other people can be a help, they can also be a hindrance. For a start, they interrupt. They interrupt in person, by phone, by text, and by e-mail. Their interruptions come in the form of questions, announcements, requests, and demands. They interrupt because they need information or advice or they want decisions to be made, conflicts managed, or problems solved.

Not only do their interruptions take up your time, but they break your focus, meaning you have to spend time re-engaging your brain so that you can carry on with what you were doing.

Although they may feel like they're not in your control, interruptions *can* be managed. To start with, accept that interruptions *will* happen. Then plan for them. This means leaving gaps in your day for interruptions;

maybe 10–20% of your time for interruptions and other delays.

Next, recognize that other people will interrupt you only if they know that you'll respond. The American writer Mark Twain decreed that his children could only get attention by blowing a horn in the direction of his back-yard studio, and only when absolutely necessary. This might be taking things a bit far, but the principle still applies; set times that you're available to deal with other people's problems and questions. And if you know that the afternoon, for example, is your most productive time of day, don't allow yourself to be interrupted then. Put the phone on answerphone.

If someone does manage to interrupt you with a query, tell the person that you'll you get back to them at a spe-cific time later that day when you're free to give it your full attention. But if you really can't avoid interruptions, then deal with each interruption one at a time. Give your full attention to each person and each query or problem. That way, you will be less stressed and more able to deal patiently, calmly, and fully with every person who needs your time.

Deal With 'Decision Leeches'

Have you been taking too much responsibility for deci-sion making? If you're in a supervisory or management position, it's inevitable that more often than not making a final choice is going to fall to you. But often, other people offload decision making onto you when, in fact, they are more than capable of making a decision themselves.

Decisions drain your time and mental energy, but how can you get others to do their fair share of decision-making? Try this: when someone asks for your decision on something, turn it back to them. Ask: 'What do you think would be best to do?' Imagine, for example, that you asked someone else to decide which restaurant to go to or where and when to have a meeting. Instead of making a decision, they e-mail you links to some possible choices for your opinion and for you to make a decision. Rather than spend time and mental energy considering the options, ask them to make a specific recommendation.

You might have a couple of conditions – standards by which something may be decided – but if you do, keep your requirements short. For example, your response might be 'I don't mind what restaurant we go to – as long as it's not the same place we went to last week'. Or 'As long as we can walk there'. And to a request for you to decide when to fit a meeting in, your reply might be 'I don't mind what day the meeting is, as long as there's a clear agenda'.

By delegating the decision making, you share the responsibility with other people and free yourself from something that others are capable of doing. So, when possible, encourage others to make the decisions so that only those above a certain level of importance will come to you.

Some people use a concept known as a 'decision tree'. This means that in the workplace, others can take responsibility for decisions at four different levels: root, trunk, branch, and leaf. Each level has a clear definition of what is expected and how to interact with each other regarding decision making. So, someone making a leaf decision doesn't have to check with anyone before making it and taking action. While a trunk decision allows a person to make the decision as long as they check with someone before going ahead.

Leaf decisions: Make the decision. Act on it. Do not report the action you took.

Branch decisions: Make the decision. Act on it. Report the action you took daily, weekly, or monthly.

Trunk decisions: Make the decision. Report your decision before you take the action.

Root decisions: Make the decision jointly, with input from others.

The analogy of root, trunk, branch, and leaf indicates the impact of a decision taken at each level. A trunk decision is not necessarily more important than a leaf decision, but if a leaf falls off a tree, the tree won't suffer. An inappropriate decision at the root level, however, can cause major problems!

Avoid Unnecessary Meetings

'If you had to identify, in one word, the reason why the human race has not achieved and never will achieve its full potential, that word would be "meetings."'

Dave Barry. American humourist.

Does your job require you to attend a lot of meetings? Are they all really necessary? Perhaps there are times when you feel like you spend more time sitting in unproductive meetings than actually working? The answer? Leave a meeting early or don't go to it in the first place. It may be a bold move, but if you've nothing to contribute and nothing to gain, why let it use up your time and stop you from getting more important or interesting things done?

You don't need to avoid all meetings, just keep the useful ones and cut out those that aren't. How do you identify the meetings to which you will have something worthwhile to contribute or gain? Ask yourself the following questions:

Is there a clear agenda; a framework to structure the meeting? Are you clear what the purpose of the meeting is? Is it, for example, to learn about a new project, to generate ideas, to make an important decision, or resolve a problem? If you're invited to a meeting that doesn't have an agenda, ask the organizer if they could provide one so that you can decide if it's going to cover anything that's important and relevant to you and your work. If not, recognize that this meeting is not going to be the best use of your time and decline the invitation.

Would a short one-to-one conversation be better? Is there an hour meeting scheduled to discuss something that would take a 10-minute discussion or an e-mail to sort out? If so, talk to the person face to face, by phone, or exchange some e-mails.

Is your entire team going to a meeting that doesn't directly impact you all? If so, suggest that just one of you attends and they can brief everyone else later.

It *is* possible to say no to a meeting. Think carefully about which ones are absolutely necessary – and which you can let go of. If you *do* have to go to the meeting, ask yourself these questions:

Is the agenda actionable? A productive meeting has an actionable agenda, which defines the desired outcomes of the meeting. If it doesn't have an actionable agenda but you can't skip the meeting, steer it in the right direction by suggesting you all identify actions that will follow as a result of the meeting.

Is the meeting veering off subject? Getting off the subject is probably the number one challenge to meeting productivity; agenda items are left untouched. If someone goes off on a tangent that is only marginally related to the designated topic and the person chairing the meeting doesn't intervene, you might have to. Simply say 'I'm concerned we're not going to have enough time for this – could we get back to the main subject?'

Can I leave early? Don't be afraid to cut it short; if the meeting is dragging on and there's nothing on the agenda that you need to be there for, excuse yourself and leave.

Say No

Learn to say 'no' to requests or tasks if you're too busy, if it is not that important, if someone else can handle it, or if it can be done later. Being able to turn other people down is a key skill that will help you manage other people's requests, demands, and interruptions. Saying no to unimportant things – unnecessary meetings or extra work – means that you can say yes to important things; the things you want to do, need doing, and that you like doing; the things that enable you to be productive.

Be clear about what you're being asked to do. If you're not sure what you're being asked to do, ask for more information so that you're clear about what's involved. And if you're not sure if you've got the time or ability, don't be afraid to ask for time to think about it before you commit yourself. Say when you'll get back to the person who's asking. If the other person says they need an answer immediately (they have a right to do this), then rather than say yes and regret it later, it's best if you say no right now.

Be honest, clear, and succinct. When you know that you don't want to do something, be clear, direct, and succinct. Simply say 'Sorry, but I'm not going to be able to do that'. Avoid waffling, rambling, or giving excuses.

Give just one reason. Don't blame someone or something else, just be honest. You only need one genuine reason for saying no. Just say what it is. Rather than say 'I'm sorry, I would do it, but I've got so much on; I can hardly think straight and I'm so behind with everything. I hope you don't mind too much. Isn't there someone else that can do it? Sorry.' Say 'I'm sorry, I'm not going to be able to ... I need the time to ...'.

Acknowledge the other person's response but stand your ground. Once you've said what you've got to say, say no more. Just listen to the other person's response. Then acknowledge their response but stand your ground. For example: 'I understand you need someone to ... (acknowledging their response) but ... I'm not going to be able to do it' (standing your ground).

Negotiate and compromise. You might, though, decide to negotiate or compromise with the other person. For example, you might say, 'I could ask someone else if they'd be prepared to ...'. Or 'I could help you at a later date'. Or 'I can't do that, but I can help you out with ... instead.'

Finally, be aware that when it comes to being productive, knowing your limits and your strengths is key to working with other people. Know your skills and strengths and make the most of them. But be aware of your limits; this means on the one hand asking for help, and on the other hand knowing when to decline other people's requests and demands.

Remember, other people can be a help or a hindrance; they can either contribute towards you getting things done or they can create problems and make things difficult. The trick is to manage the hindrances and make use of the help.

In a nutshell

- Trying to do everything yourself is not the best use of your time, skills, or energy; struggling for hours or days before finally getting help can leave you feeling overwhelmed and stressed. And then you can't do *anything* properly!
- Asking for help doesn't mean you're inadequate, it simply means that you need support and assistance with something specific for a specific amount of time.
- Asking for help – or delegating some tasks and chores – can also free you up to focus on what you – and maybe only you – can do well.
- Other people are often more willing to help than you might think. But if you don't ask, the answer is already no!
- Make it easy for someone to help you. Know what, exactly, you want help with and what needs doing. Ask the right person for their help. Ask directly. Delegate, don't dump; consider the other person's situation.
- Manage interruptions: accept that they *will* happen. Then plan for them. Don't allow yourself to be interrupted at your most productive time of day; set specific times that you are available to deal with other people's problems and questions.
- Decisions drain your time and mental energy. When someone asks for your decision on something, turn it back to them and ask them to make

a specific recommendation. You might have a couple of conditions but, if you do, keep your requirements short.

- Leave a meeting early or don't go to it in the first place. If you've nothing to contribute and nothing to gain, why let it use up your time and stop you from getting more important things done? You don't need to avoid all meetings, just keep the useful ones and cut out those that aren't.

- Learn to say 'no' to requests or tasks if you're too busy, if it is not that important, if someone else can handle it, or if it can be done later.

6
Look After Yourself

Get Moving

If you're going to give your best to being productive and getting things done, you need to aim for a balanced amount of work and rest in your life. And it's not just rest breaks you need. You also need to take frequent breaks that involve moving.

Many of us take a train, bus, or car for our commute to and from work. We spend hours at a desk, return home, and then slob out on the sofa for the evening. And we do it all sitting down.

A comprehensive review of studies on sedentary behaviour carried out by researchers from Loughborough University and the University of Leicester links sitting for lengthy periods with a range of health problems including an increased risk of heart disease, obesity, diabetes, and cancer. In 2018, The World Health Organization listed inactivity as the fourth biggest risk factor for global adult mortality. Even if you do the recommended 150 minutes (in bouts of 10 minutes or more) of moderate aerobic exercise through the week (be it a run, a gym session, or a brisk walk), if you spend long periods of every day sitting down, you're still classed as 'sedentary' and at risk of health problems.

So, if sitting is the problem, could standing be the solution? Apparently not. Whether you sit or stand, it's being in one position that's the problem.

What to do? Move more.

In 2016, the UK government publication 'Health Matters: Getting every adult active everyday' recommended that we should break up long periods of sitting time with short bouts of activity every 30 minutes. The publication suggests: 'As well as being physically active, all adults are advised to minimise the time spent being sedentary (sitting) for extended periods. Even among individuals who are active at the recommended levels, spending large amounts of time sedentary increases the risk of adverse health outcomes.' It goes on to suggest that we should reduce the amount of time we sit during our working day by taking regular time *not* sitting during work and finding ways to break up sedentary time.

So, if your work involves sitting or standing for long periods, how you can be more active? Here are a few ideas for making your working day more active.

Set a reminder. To help you get into the habit of moving more, use an app or phone reminder to prompt you to move around for a couple of minutes every 30–60 minutes.

Walk instead of calling or emailing. Pretend it's the 1990s! Instead of e-mailing, texting, or messaging a colleague across the room, walk over to their desk and talk with them face to face. Put your printer and rubbish bin on the other side of the room so you have to get up to use them. Take phone calls standing up. And use the stairs, not the lift.

Turn waiting time into moving time. Waiting to use the photocopier or for colleagues to vacate the meeting room you've booked? Don't stand there twiddling your thumbs. Take a stroll instead.

Stretch. Stand up to stretch out your chest and extend your spine to reverse the hunched position of sitting. As well as moving around, improve your posture. Activities that can help your posture include yoga, tai chi, qigong, Pilates, and the Alexander technique.

Drink more water. But don't have a bottle by your desk so you can sip throughout the day. Instead, leave it in the staff kitchen or somewhere else so that you have to get up and walk every hour or so. Don't keep food next to you either; put it somewhere that you have to get up and go to. And use the toilets furthest away from your desk.

Volunteer for the coffee run. Go out and get your coffee, tea, or smoothie instead of letting someone else pick one up for you. Try and get in a 15-minute walk at lunch. Find a new sandwich shop that's further away from the one you usually use. And find new places to eat outside. See your lunchtime as a time to get moving and to enjoy your food, not a time to stuff something from the nearest food shop down your neck.

Organize standing or walking meetings. Not only does it get you out of your chair, but it could be a good way to make sure meetings are more efficient and don't drag on unnecessarily.

Not everyone can get moving in this way if they are a wheelchair user or have other mobility problems. Matthew McCarthy, a researcher at the University of Leicester's Department of Cardiovascular Sciences, suggests that 'completing short bursts of upper body activities using resistance bands or table-top arm cranks' may be a way to activate your muscles and get moving.

As well as moving around every 30–60 minutes there's other things you can do to make your working day more active:

Walk, run, or cycle at least part of the way to and from work. If you can bike, walk, or even run to work, this can be an excellent way to fit more activity into your day. Even if you don't live close enough to your workplace to be able to do this, you can still find ways to make at least part of your journey more active. Get the train part of the way and ride the rest, get off the bus a few stops early and walk, or park your car a kilometre or two away or find the furthest carpark space from your workplace building.

Start an office fitness challenge. Get your colleagues involved and make it a challenge to be more active together. As well as the physical health benefits, regular bouts of activity can help boost productivity. When you're moving, you are also increasing blood flow to the brain, which can help you stay alert and on top of things.

Take a hike: It's well known that walking helps improve oxygen flow to the brain; we only need to walk at a moderate pace to increase our heart rate which then causes us to breathe deeper which, in turn, helps more oxygen get into the bloodstream. With the heart pumping faster, our circulation increases and more oxygen gets to the brain.

But new research has suggested that it's not just our hearts that are responsible for blood flow to the brain. Researchers at New Mexico Highlands University have recently found that the impact from your feet hitting the ground while walking sends a hydraulic wave upward through your body. This wave is actually strong enough to send blood back up through your arteries, increasing blood flow to the brain. While the effects of walking on cerebral blood flow (CBF) were less dramatic than those caused by running, they were greater than the effects seen during cycling, which involves no foot impact at all.

More oxygen getting to the brain is a good thing. Your brain uses about 20% of your body's total oxygen supply, so if you're not getting enough oxygen up there, it's easy to feel groggy and unfocused. You don't need to start running marathons! You can start by simply going for a brisk walk at lunch.

Switch Off

No matter how active your day, creating a balance between working and not working is essential when it comes to being happy and productive. Sometimes it can feel like work is taking over your life. It's not just that you spend most of your day at work; even when you're not there, you're still thinking about it. With constant access to the internet, email, and texts, it's easy to stay plugged in all day when you're at work and when you're away from it. You can find yourself in a state of permanent activity with little in the way of a rest or break when technology puts you somewhere that you're not.

You need to switch off! Just as you wouldn't leave the engine of your car running when it's parked outside, so you need to switch off the engine of your mind. Here are a few ways to switch off and leave work behind:

Get closure; leave work at work. Before you leave work, empty your head. Simply write a note or e-mail to yourself of any work-related things that are on your mind; tasks left to do and any concerns. Then shut the notebook, turn off your computer, and walk away.

Quit while you're ahead. Use Ernest Hemingway's approach: 'I always worked until I had something done and I always stopped when I knew what was going to happen next. That way I could be sure of going on the next day.' Stopping while you're ahead is a good tactic: you know what you've done, you know exactly what you'll do next, and you feel fine about getting started again.

Set a firm cut-off time. To get you out of work by, say 5 or 6 p.m., plan something – an activity or event or a totally separate, unrelated task for after work. Meeting up with a friend for a drink, booking an exercise class, or stopping to make dinner creates a different obligation to attend and moves you away from work.

Close the door on it. If you do need to bring work home, if possible only work in a specific room in your home so that when you're done, you can close the door on it. Unless your job specifically requires you to be on call 24/7, there's little that happens after 8 p.m. that can't wait until the morning.

Disconnect. On your days off, consider having a full day or at least a few hours to disconnect. Get used to being without your phone, tablet, or laptop. Get some fresh air. Go hiking or cycling. Play a sport. Take a phone but turn it off. Do something creative, artistic, or musical.

Avoid burnout. Whether it's stress, constant bouts of illnesses due to a weakened immune system, or constant exhaustion, recognize the early warning signs before you start burning out. Don't ignore the signs. Overwhelmed? Get some advice and support. Feeling tired? Get more sleep. Getting ill? Take time off.

Your body and mind need rest to function properly. Taking time to recharge is crucial to sustaining motivation, perseverance, and productivity. Think of it this way: anything that increases your ability to be efficient and productive is part of your job. Anything that reduces your ability to be efficient and productive is part of your job to not do.

In a nutshell

- Move more! Take frequent breaks that involve moving.
- As well as moving around every 30–60 minutes, find a way to make your working day more active.
- Creating a balance between working and not working is essential when it comes to being happy and productive.
- Switch off! Your body and mind need rest to function properly. Taking time to recharge is crucial to sustaining motivation, perseverance, and productivity.

About The Author

Gill Hasson is a teacher, trainer, and writer. She has 20 years' experience in the area of personal development. Her expertise is in the areas of confidence and self-esteem, communication skills, assertiveness, and resilience.

Gill delivers teaching and training for educational organizations, voluntary and business organizations, and the public sector.

Gill is the author of the bestselling *Mindfulness* and *Emotional Intelligence* plus other books on the subjects of dealing with difficult people, resilience, communication skills, and assertiveness.

Gill's particular interest and motivation is in helping people to realize their potential, to live their best life! You can contact Gill via her website at www.gillhasson .co.uk or e-mail her at gillhasson@btinternet.com.

Index

Index

Index